Written by Meike Roth-Beck

Illustrated by Klaus Ensikat

Translated by Laura Watkinson

Eerdmans Books for Young Readers

Grand Rapids, Michigan

The Life and Times of Martin Luther

IN THE YEAR 1517 . . .

. . . a man became famous. So famous that even five hundred years later, many people still associate that year with his name—Martin Luther.

Of course, there was no way Luther could have guessed he would become so famous. He was simply a thirty-three-year-old theology professor in the small German town of Wittenberg.

But in 1517, Martin Luther published his Ninety-Five Theses, setting an unstoppable chain of events in motion.

This book tells his story.

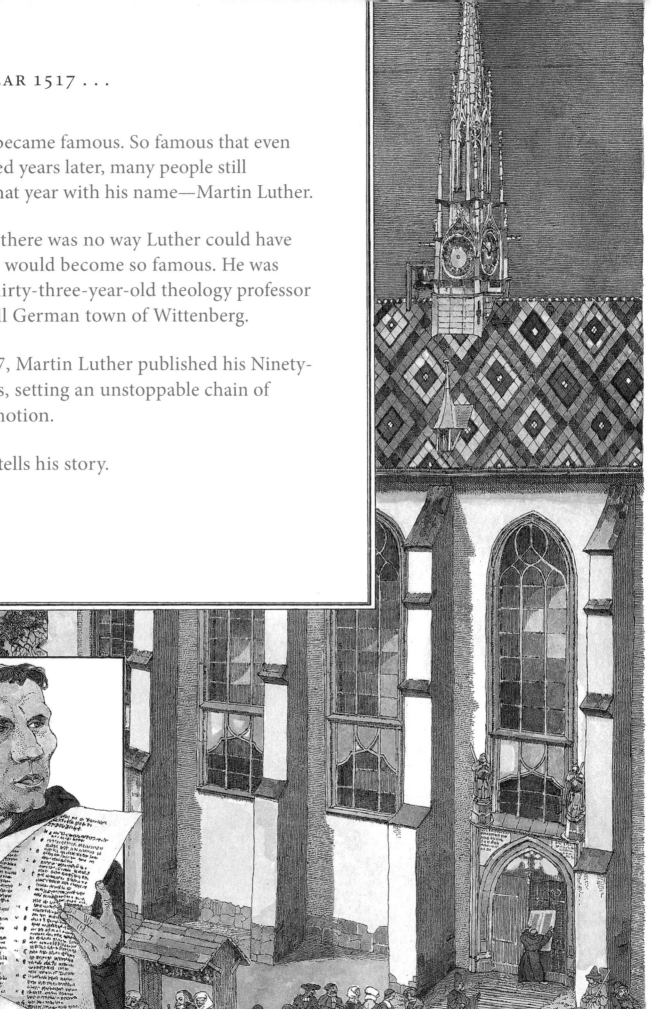

Martin Luther was born into a world where life was very different than it is today.

In the Middle Ages, people suffered because of drought, flooding, and crop failure. A terrible disease, the plague, spread across Europe, taking many lives. During this time, there was only one church in Europe, the Catholic Church, and leaving its protection was unimaginable. The pope in Rome was considered the unchallenged representative of God on earth, and bishops throughout Europe followed his orders. People who questioned the teachings of the Church, who developed new ideas and wanted to investigate nature and the world,

EMPEROR MAXIMILIAN I

were persecuted without mercy. Some of them were even burned alive for disagreeing with the Church.

However, in the late fifteenth century, this established order started to crumble. The emperor and the pope began to lose their power and influence. Some people, filled with curiosity and a thirst for knowledge, wanted to know more than what they were learning from the Church. Universities were founded, new technologies were invented, and the human body was studied down to the last detail. When Christopher Columbus sailed from Spain in 1492, Martin Luther was eight years old.

POPE LEO X

EISLEBEN

How it all began

Martin Luther was born on November 10, 1483, to Hans and Margarete Luther, in the small town of Eisleben in central Germany. The day after his birth, on Saint Martin's Day, he was baptized and named after Saint Martin of Tours, a Roman soldier who shared his cloak with a beggar and who is still revered to this day.

Every year in November, two great men are remembered, both of them named Martin. People gather in marketplaces to celebrate and make music and tell stories. Children sing and walk in parades through the streets, carrying homemade lanterns. Neither Saint Martin of Tours nor Martin Luther should be forgotten.

MINING

THE EARLY YEARS

Martin was the oldest of nine children. When he was a young boy, the family moved to Mansfeld, where his father worked in the mining industry. Over the years, Martin's father earned a considerable fortune, becoming a mine owner and a respected citizen. Martin's parents wanted to make sure their son received a good education. They were certain that he had the potential to do something important with his life.

When Martin was fifteen years old, his parents sent him to school in Eisenach, a town some distance away. He was a very good student and eager to learn. Martin was particularly enthusiastic about music and poetry, and he loved to sing and play the lute. Later he even composed hymns that are still sung in churches today. Two of his most famous hymns are "A Mighty Fortress Is Our God" and "From Heaven Above to Earth I Come."

The young Luther was fortunate to be able to live with the Cotta family, who were well-respected merchants. He was well fed, and he learned much about the world, since the family was visited by many guests who had traveled to distant lands.

In Eisenach

Whenever Martin left the Cotta family's house, he could see Saint George's Church, where he sang in the church choir. The church was an old and important one. Three hundred years before Luther's time, a young princess had been married there—Saint Elizabeth of Hungary, as she was later known. She was married to the Count of Thuringia and lived at the famous Wartburg Castle. This saintly woman often left her castle and went into town to help the poor and nurse the sick.

Saint Elizabeth's bones were revered in Luther's day. Faithful believers would go on long pilgrimages, hoping to feel divine power from such relics, as they were called. That was what the church taught and what the young Martin and other students learned.

The small town of Eisenach was full of God-fearing monks, nuns, and priests, but Martin's parents wanted a different life for their son. They hoped that Martin would become a lawyer, find respectable work, and earn a good living. So when Martin was seventeen, his mother and father sent him to the university in Erfurt. A great future lay ahead of him; all he had to do was seize the opportunity.

While he was studying in Erfurt, Martin often visited his parents in Mansfeld. It was a long walk, which took several days.

One day in 1505, on his way back to Erfurt, Martin was caught in a furious thunderstorm. A lightning bolt struck near him. Thunder rumbled and lightning flashed as if it were the end of the world. He was terrified. In desperation, he called out, "Help me, Saint Anne, and I will become a monk." As if by a miracle, he made it through the storm unharmed—and he did not forget what he had promised Saint Anne, the patron saint of miners, in his time of great need.

Martin kept his word. He gave away his belongings to his friends and, two weeks after the storm, he entered the Augustinian monastery in Erfurt to become a monk. He exchanged his clothes for a coarsely woven black robe and, like all monks, led a life following strict rules and regulations.

His parents could not believe it. They were horrified. Was this the end of the story for their son? Martin's education had cost so much money. And now he was going to spend the rest of his life praying and fasting? But Martin had made up his mind, and he stayed at the monastery. Every day was the same, with a rhythm set by regular prayer. Martin did not have a room of his own or any personal belongings. His bed was a simple sack of straw. He soon took his vows and became a monk, promising to be obedient and poor, and not to marry.

Martin used every spare minute to study the Bible. He prepared to be ordained as a priest, which involved holding a service to show everyone he was now a man of the Church. When the day came, he celebrated his first Mass. It was a very solemn occasion. Martin could hardly believe it: even his father came, although he had never visited Martin at the monastery. He gave his son a gift of money, though he still could not forgive him.

Martin had done it. He was now a priest. But although he diligently followed the monastic rules, he still doubted God's love for him. This worry would not let him rest, and it followed him for the next few years . . .

Becoming a priest was not enough for Martin Luther. He wanted to study theology, and he was able to do that in Wittenberg. By 1510, he had become so respected that he was given an important task: to travel to Rome to meet with representatives of the pope. It was a great honor.

First he had to undertake a long and difficult journey across the Alps on foot. Together with another monk, Luther set off on his journey. They traveled for many weeks, across Germany, Switzerland, and Italy, until they finally saw Rome in the distance. He had dreamed about this for so long. Maybe he would even meet the pope! Luther was overwhelmed. He fell to his knees and cried out, "Greetings to you, holy Rome!"

But what he experienced in that city left Luther shocked and confused. So-called letters of indulgence were being sold on every corner. The Church taught that anyone who bought such a document purchased forgiveness for their sins. Luther himself bought a letter of indulgence, like so many other pilgrims to Rome. He found it disturbing, though, that the Church seemed to be working tirelessly to bring in money when it was already so rich. Of course, the construction of the magnificent Saint Peter's Basilica was expensive. But was it right to sell indulgences? When Martin returned to Germany, this question would burn within him until he found an answer.

Martin Luther confided his questions and doubts to his friend Johann von Staupitz, the leader of the Augustinian friars and a dean at the University of Wittenberg. Johann also knew the question that was troubling Luther: What does a Christian believer have to do to be loved by God? To Luther's surprise, Johann offered him a position as theology professor at the University of Wittenberg. "Study, teach, preach!" he urged. And so the inquisitive, doubting monk became a professor of theology.

Finally, one day in 1515, while reading the Bible, Luther came upon an answer: God's love does not have to be earned. It is a gift that each

person only has to accept. Luther's doubts about God's love vanished; he was finally free.

His enthusiasm was contagious. More and more young people came to Wittenberg to study with him. They liked what Martin Luther had to say about Christianity, and they also appreciated how he dared to question the teachings of the Church. He not only taught what the Church said, but also emphasized what was in the Bible. His way of thinking shocked some people but also found support. Martin Luther had become a respected theologian.

MONK'S CELL

Preachers had been sent everywhere—even to Wittenberg—to collect money for Saint Peter's Basilica in Rome. One of these men was Johann Tetzel. Martin Luther knew that the people of Wittenberg had long been buying letters of indulgence from Tetzel to free themselves from their sins. Luther refused to accept this anymore.

So he wrote down a long list of the ideas that were on his mind, ending up with ninety-five thoughts in total. He wrote about the meaning of penance and confession, about his opinion on the sale of indulgences, about the construction of Saint Peter's, and about the preachers who were collecting money. An academic like Luther refers to such key thoughts as "theses."

He set off for the Castle Church in Wittenberg, where he nailed his ninety-five theses to the door. Now everyone could read them!

Thanks to a relatively new invention, the printing press, Luther's theses were quickly reproduced and distributed. They spread like wildfire and were soon known far beyond Wittenberg. It was not only powerful bishops who pricked up their ears. Even the pope in far-off Rome heard about Luther's theses.

Luther was playing with fire, but he still continued to state his opinions freely. He signed his letters as "Martin Luther, the liberated man." He also used a special seal, the Luther rose. At its center was a heart with a cross.
He wanted to show everyone how important
his faith in a merciful God was to him.

Some of the theses explained

In the introduction to his theses, Martin Luther called for an open discussion of his ideas.

Professor Dr. Martin Luther announces: All are invited to join me in the search for truth! I would like to start with the following theses. Those who wish to join the discussion, but are not in Wittenberg, may send a letter. In the name of our Lord Jesus Christ, Amen.

When Jesus told his followers to repent, he meant that they should live their whole lives in repentance. (Thesis 1)

Luther found in the Bible what Jesus thought about penance, or seeking forgiveness. The Bible doesn't say anything about buying letters of indulgence to earn God's forgiveness. Penance means living differently than usual, more attentively, more quietly—perhaps even so quietly that we learn to hear God. This idea was so important to Luther that he placed it right at the beginning of his list.

GRACE—A GIFT

Any Christian who truly repents has the right to have their sins fully forgiven, even without letters of indulgence. (Thesis 36)

Luther didn't object to people confessing to a priest when they had done something wrong. And he believed the Church could suggest actions that would help people make things right: they could pray, fast, give money to those in need, or go on pilgrimages to holy sites. But Luther wanted it to be clear that the Church could only make these suggestions. It did not have the power to forgive sin. Only God could do that.

No one but God can look into people's hearts and know if they truly repent. Luther believed that anyone could put things right with God—without the pope and without the Church. No one needs to pay money in order to earn God's love. God's love is a gift, and we need only to accept it. Luther called this gift "grace."

Christians should be taught that whoever sees other people in need and does not help them, but instead spends money on indulgences, is not buying God's forgiveness, but God's anger. (Thesis 45)

Christians should be taught that those who have little to spare should use their money to provide for their families, and not squander it on indulgences. (Thesis 46)

Christians should be taught that buying indulgences is their own choice—it is not commanded. (Thesis 47)

Martin Luther was angry that the priests who sold indulgences would frighten people, even the very poorest, into parting with their money.

It was easy for those with fat purses to part with their money. They could try to buy the right to a place in heaven and believe themselves safe. But the people who didn't have much money lived in fear of ending up in Purgatory, the place of suffering that indulgence sellers warned them about. What else could they do but give away their last coins for letters of indulgence? That couldn't be right!

INDULGENCES FOR THE DEAD

Whoever preaches that "When the coin in the coffer rings, the soul from purgatory springs!" isn't teaching something that comes from God—but from humans. (Thesis 27)

Martin Luther was outraged that people had been told that they could save even the dead from Purgatory if only they bought indulgences. In truth, this was just a story made up by people.

The pope and Saint Peter's Basilica

Christians should be taught that the pope needs their devout prayers much more than he needs their money. (Thesis 48)

Christians should be taught that if the pope knew how the indulgence preachers were frightening poor people into giving up their money, he would sooner see Saint Peter's Basilica burned to the ground than see it built with the skin, flesh, and bones of those who look up to him. (Thesis 50)

Christians should be taught that the pope would gladly give up his own money—even sell Saint Peter's—to help the poor people from whom the indulgence-sellers are taking money. (Thesis 51)

Local church leaders should welcome messengers from Rome with respect, but they should also pay close attention to make sure that they preach what the pope has instructed, and not their own message. (Theses 69 and 70)

Martin Luther was good at pointing out the Church's abuses without directly attacking the pope. Even so, he wrote very clearly about what needed to change.

The Church and its good news

It is not good when preachers spend more time in their sermons talking about indulgences than they do about the word of God. (Thesis 54)

Surely the pope believes that if an insignificant indulgence is celebrated with a single bell or parade or ceremony, then the gospel, which is the very greatest thing, should be celebrated with hundreds of bells, parades, and ceremonies. (Thesis 55)

The Church's true treasure is the holy gospel of the glory and grace of God. (Thesis 62)

The Church once used the treasure of the gospel to draw people in, like a net for catching fish. But now the Church is instead using the treasure of indulgences as a net to fish for people's money. (Theses 65 and 66)

Martin Luther cared deeply about the Church. He was troubled that, in thinking only about money, it had forgotten its task—to preach the good news that Jesus taught and showed by his example. Jesus took care of the sick, the homeless, the foreigner, and all those who were burdened. He especially gave children the loving attention they needed. He taught that every single person is important to God.

WHAT DO PEOPLE WANT TO KNOW?

The people want to know why God and the pope will allow a wicked person to purchase forgiveness for a good and righteous person who has died. Shouldn't they rather—out of pure love—offer that forgiveness free of charge? (Thesis 84)

The people also want to know why the pope doesn't build Saint Peter's with his own vast wealth, rather than using the money of poor Christians. (Thesis 86)

The people deserve answers to these questions and complaints. Silencing them by force will only make Christians unhappy, and give enemies of the Church and the pope a reason to disrespect them. (Thesis 90)

Martin Luther listened to people on the streets talking among themselves. Many of them were also dissatisfied with the Church. His theses drew attention to their legitimate questions.

THE FINAL THESIS

Christians should be encouraged to be faithful in following Jesus Christ, their true leader, no matter the difficulty. Then they can be confident of entering heaven, without having to place their trust in a false hope. (Theses 94 and 95)

Martin Luther sensed that a time had come when people were starting to take control of their own lives. The Church could not take that away from them, and it could not promise them a place in heaven.

By presenting his theses, Luther bravely set in motion a chain of events that could not be stopped. What happened next was out of his hands.

Less than a year later, Martin Luther was summoned to Rome by the pope to explain why he had written his theses. Frederick III, known as Frederick the Wise, the founder of the University of Wittenberg, was wary of this interrogation and didn't want one of his most famous professors placed at risk. He arranged for the questioning to take place in Augsburg instead of Rome, so he would be better able to protect Luther.

In Augsburg, Cardinal Cajetan, the pope's representative, demanded that Luther withdraw his theses and stop interfering in Church matters.

FREDERICK III

Luther, however, would not consider taking back any of his statements. This put him in great danger. The cardinal tried to have him arrested, but Luther escaped at night through a small gate that the mayor's son had shown him, and got away safely.

But the dispute was far from over. Luther grew ever more dissatisfied with the teachings of the Church, finally declaring that even the Church could be wrong, and so could the pope. For the Catholic Church, this was the final straw. How could Martin Luther dare to question the decisions of the Catholic Church?

Banished from the Church

The pope sent Luther a letter threatening to banish him from the Church. Instead of being intimidated, Luther responded by burning the letter, together with other Church writings, in front of the city gate in Wittenberg. The pope and the emperor agreed: Martin Luther was a dangerous troublemaker. He had to go.

Although this sealed Luther's exclusion from the Church, in 1521 Emperor Charles V still summoned him to attend the Imperial Diet, an assembly of various authorities, in the town of Worms, where representatives of the Church, the towns, and a number of princes came together for discussion. They all agreed: Luther had already infected too many people with his dangerous opinions. He had to be silenced.

Luther knew that his life was at risk. After all, the theology professor Jan Hus had spoken out against indulgences and been burned at the stake for heresy a hundred years earlier. Luther fretted over what to do. Did he have any choice? With mixed emotions, he set off for Worms to present himself for questioning.

34

Luther traveled for two weeks to reach Worms. On the way there, he preached in Gotha, Erfurt, and Eisenach, and he was welcomed enthusiastically wherever he went.

When Luther reached Worms, he was called before the emperor and ordered to recant his teachings and writings. But he stood by his words. He based his arguments on his faith, the Bible, his conscience, and his reason. He is said to have spoken these famous words: "Here I stand. I can do no other! God help me. Amen."

As a result, the emperor declared an "imperial ban" on Luther, making him an outlaw, which

EMPEROR CHARLES V

meant anyone could kill him without any legal consequences. Luther was in grave danger. The emperor had promised him safe conduct for twenty-one days. But what then?

Frederick the Wise had already decided: Martin Luther had to be rescued. Frederick arranged for Luther to be kidnapped in the Thuringian Forest. It looked as if Luther had been abducted, and maybe even murdered, by highwaymen.

In reality, though, he was well hidden at Wartburg Castle. He disguised himself as a knight, calling himself "Sir George." Everyone would think he was dead, and no longer a danger to the pope and the emperor. The plan worked.

Martin Luther made good use of his time, translating the New Testament into good, clear German that everyone could understand. He wanted all Christians to be able to read the Bible, not only the educated churchmen. He worked day and night to complete his ambitious project. It took him only eleven weeks. Luther tried to write his translation the way people really spoke. He wanted to make sure the meaning was clear to everyone.

Finally, in 1522, Luther dared to come out of his hiding place and return to Wittenberg. He wanted some changes to occur within the Church. Luther thought that everyone should be able to read the Bible and learn from it. And he wanted more church services held in German instead of Latin, so that people could understand what was being said.

Luther had his work cut out for him, but he also had many friends to help and advise him. One such friend was the scholar Philipp Melanchthon, who also devised new systems of education. More and more supporters, even rulers, became convinced by Luther's arguments and echoed his call for a "Reformation," a modernization of the Church.

PHILIPP MELANCHTHON   CASPAR CRUCIGER   LUTHER   JUSTUS JONAS   JOHANNES BUGENHAGEN

The stories of Martin Luther's words and deeds made it all the way to a remote convent several days' journey from Wittenberg. The nuns who lived there, isolated from the world, were amazed to read Martin Luther's writings. Could they really choose to leave the convent, even though the Catholic Church forbade it? In a secret letter, they asked Luther for help. Luther agreed. One night in 1523, a merchant friend of Luther's not only delivered his barrels of herring; he also hid some nuns from the convent in his covered wagon. After a dangerous and difficult journey, all of the women arrived safely in Wittenberg. The clever and beautiful Katharina von Bora was one of them.

Katharina was twenty-four years old and all alone in Wittenberg. However, the famous painter Lucas Cranach soon offered to let her stay with his family. Even so, as a young woman who had chosen to leave the convent, she needed to find a husband. While the other nuns who had escaped soon married, the head-strong Katharina rejected a number of suitors. Finally, in 1525, Martin Luther himself took Katharina von Bora as his wife.

For a long time, Luther and his wife had to put up with mockery and gossip. Even Philipp Melanchthon, one of Luther's closest companions, did not approve of his friend's marriage. But Luther stood firm. By getting married, he was showing the pope and the whole world that a man of the Church could have a wife and family.

Martin and Katharina lived at the so-called "Black Cloister" in Wittenberg. They had six children: Johannes, Elisabeth, Magdalena, Martin, Paul, and Margarethe. There was always a lot of hustle and bustle in their welcoming home. Katharina was an industrious woman who not only took good care of her large family, but also devoted attention and energy to her house, garden, and estate. Luther affectionately called her "Mister Kate."

Martin Luther and Katharina von Bora became a model for clerical marriage. That remains the case even today.

Luther, together with his friend Philipp Melanchthon, achieved more than anyone would ever have dared to think. In 1530, the two men wrote their own creed, which is known today as the Augsburg Confession.

In 1534, the first Bible printed in the German language came out, allowing it to be read by ordinary people. Luther continued to work hard, neglecting his health. He wrote, preached, taught, and helped to reform the Church.

In 1546, at the age of 62, Martin Luther died while on a journey to Eisleben, the very town where he was born. Luther was buried in the Castle Church at Wittenberg, the place where he had inspired so many people.

Martin Luther's teachings resulted in great divisions and even wars, and it took a long time for religious peace to come to Europe. Luther himself did not live to see that day. Today, letters of indulgence have long since been abolished, and Christians strive for peace and justice throughout the world. With more than two billion followers, Christianity is the largest religious community in the world. Seventy-four million of those Christians are Lutherans. It is still important to them that God is merciful. No one has to earn God's love. It is a gift.

Every year on October 31, Reformation Day, we are reminded of everything that Martin Luther started when he published his Ninety-Five Theses in 1517.

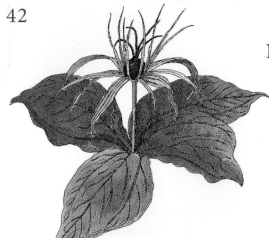

Notes on the illustrations

p. 1: The swan has become a symbol of Luther. This is usually explained by the following story: In 1415, the Prague reformer Jan Hus was executed as a heretic. Before he was burned at the stake, he supposedly said, "Today you are roasting a goose, but a swan will rise from the ashes" (the Czech word *husa* means "goose"). The image of the swan Hus spoke about was later linked to Luther.

pp. 4–5: The Castle Church in Wittenberg, where Luther is said to have nailed his theses to the door. The theses were intended to spark an academic debate among theologians. The tower canopies have only existed since the middle of the sixteenth century.

p. 6: Emperor Maximilian I, ruler from 1493 to 1519, one of the major secular authorities during Luther's time.

p. 7: Pope Leo X, born Giovanni de' Medici, pope from 1513 to 1521, and the major religious authority during Luther's time.

p. 10: Mining scene, as depicted in the Annaberg mining altar by painter Hans Hesse in 1522. One of the elements is a smelting hut with smoke issuing from it. Luther's father owned several such smelteries.

p. 12: Saint Elizabeth of Hungary (1207–1231), depicted here in St. George's Church. Legend has it that she was taken by surprise on her way to give bread to the poor, which was forbidden. Miraculously, the bread turned into roses. On the lower right is the house of the Cotta family (now the Lutherhaus in Eisenach). Eisenach was also the birthplace of renowned Baroque composer Johann Sebastian Bach.

p. 13: The "Collegium Maius," the Old University in Erfurt, today the administrative headquarters for the Protestant Church in Central Germany.

p. 18: On the right is Johann von Staupitz (c. 1460–1524), based on an engraving from 1889.

p. 20: The Dominican friar Johann Tetzel (1465–1519) is holding a skull as a *memento mori* (reminder of death). The wooden panel on the pulpit shows the Medici family crest, the personal coat of arms of Pope Leo X.

p. 21: This picture of the Luther rose was taken from the original tomb of Martin Luther in the Church of St. Michael in Jena. Luther himself developed the rose based on his family coat of arms, and later interpreted its colors symbolically. The rose became the symbol of his theology.

p. 30: Frederick III (1463–1525), known as Frederick the Wise, Elector of Saxony, and Georg Spalatin (1484–1545), secretary, librarian, and tutor to princes, are depicted here, with Pope Leo X in the upper left.

p. 31: Augsburg Cathedral and the hearing in Augsburg. Cardinal Thomas Cajetan (1469–1534), the pope's representative, is shown wearing the red cap; the man with raised finger is Bavarian politician Dr. Leonhard von Eck (1480–1550).

p. 32: Burning of the papal decree or "bull" along with other legal documents of the Catholic Church. Luther is wearing a doctoral cap.

p. 34: Top left: The imperial herald Kaspar Sturm (1475–1552), in his heraldic garment with the emblem of an eagle, as he accompanies Luther to Worms. Bottom: The young Emperor Charles V (1500–1558) declares the imperial ban on Luther.

p. 39: Luther's home—a former monastery, known as the Black Cloister, or the Black Monastery, because of the Augustinian monks' black robes.

p. 41: A replica of the printing press pictured here is on display at the Albrecht Dürer House in Nuremberg. Top right: One of the first Protestant churches, St. Anne's Church in Augsburg.

Meike Roth-Beck is an author and editor for radio broadcasters and educational publishing houses. Previously, she worked as an adult education teacher and an educator for the Protestant Church in Central Germany. She lives with her family in Eisenach.

Klaus Ensikat is one of Germany's most beloved illustrators. His artwork has earned him many prestigious awards, including the Hans Christian Andersen Award for illustration, which commemorates his lifetime achievements.

First published in the United States in 2017
by Eerdmans Books for Young Readers,
an imprint of Wm. B. Eerdmans Publishing Co.
2140 Oak Industrial Dr. NE, Grand Rapids, Michigan 49505

www.eerdmans.com/youngreaders

Originally published in Germany in 2015 under the title
Von Martin Luthers Wittenberger Thesen by Kindermann Verlag
Theodor-Heuss-Platz 6
D-14052 Berlin, Germany
www.kindermannverlag.de

Text copyright © 2015 Meike Roth-Beck
Illustrations copyright © 2015 Klaus Ensikat
© Kindermann Verlag, 2015
English-language translation © 2017 Laura Watkinson

23 22 21 20 19 18 17   1 2 3 4 5 6 7 8 9

ISBN 978-0-8028-5495-7
Manufactured in Malaysia

A catalog record of this book is available from the Library of Congress.

FSC
www.fsc.org

MIX
Paper from
responsible sources
FSC® C012700